DOROTHY HAMILL

SKATE TO VICTORY

DOROTHY HAMILL

SKATE TO VICTORY

By Dorothy Childers Schmitz

Library of Congress Catalog Card Number: 77-70888. International Standard Book Number: 0-913940-62-3.

Design - Doris Woods and Randal M. Heise

PHOTOGRAPHIC CREDITS

David Leonardi: 5, 7, 8, 11, 12, 15, 16,
18, 20, 22, 25, 26A, B, C, 28, 31, Cover, 32, 35, 36, 44
United Press International: 41, 42, 47
Wide World: 3

DOROTHY HAMILL

SKATE TO VICTORY

It all began with a pair of skates for Christmas.

Dorothy Hamill was eight years old when she stood on the ice for the first time. It was like any other winter afternoon at the local pond. Children laughed and played on the ice. Dorothy learned to stand on her new skates that day. But mostly she laughed and had fun with her friends.

It was fun. She loved it. She watched some of the older children skate backwards. "I want to learn to do that," she thought.

Dorothy went home from the frozen pond and told her parents, "I want to learn to skate backwards. Skating is fun," she said.

One day she saw a skater doing spins on TV. "I want to learn all that," she said.

Dorothy skated every time she could. Her mother and father saw how much she enjoyed it. They decided she could take lessons.

The next weekend, her mother took her to an ice rink for some lessons. After that they went to the rink often. The more Dorothy skated, the better she became. And the more she liked it.

By spring, her skating teacher could see that Dorothy was going to be a very good skater. Soon she was going to the rink every day to practice. Skating became more important to her than school or anything else.

That summer, Dorothy had more time than ever to skate. She had even worn out that pair of skates she got for Christmas! So with another brand new pair of skates, she became even more determined to be the best in her skating class.

One day her teacher told her that she was ready to take the test.

"What test?" Dorothy asked. Her teacher answered, "It's the first of a series of tests to show how much your skating improves."

Her teacher explained that the tests were set up by the United States Figure Skating Association. Skaters learn to skate certain figures in each test. Then they move on to the next test when they learn the next figures. The figures get harder every time. "Some skaters skate just for fun," she said. "But some want to enter contests and competitions. So they learn the figures and take the tests."

Dorothy thought about all her teacher had told her. "Yes," she said. "I want to do it." That December she passed the first of eight tests - only a year after she got her first skates for Christmas.

Then Dorothy began to get ready for her second test. She learned the new figures. She did not mind getting up early to go to the rink. She practiced those figures until she was ready. Then she took the second test.

By the next December, she was ready for her first competition. The contest was called the North Atlantic Regionals. And she was only ten years old. She entered the contest and finished in eighth place.

She decided to practice even more. When the local rinks were too crowded, her mother would take her to other rinks to practice.

Soon Dorothy was ready for her third test. Then the fourth. All this practice meant that she was away from home much of the time. She joined a figure skating club in Rye, New York. In a contest there, she won some free lessons. Dorothy and her mother spent much of their time going back and forth to the rinks so she could practice and compete.

Dorothy practices during Christmas vacation at Lake Placid.

Dorothy concentrates on her school figures.

One cold Saturday morning, Dorothy's mother could not drive her to the rink. So she set out walking. It would have taken her hours to get there in the freezing cold. When her mother found that she was gone, she went looking for her. She found her and took her to the rink. Now her mother really knew how much skating meant to her.

Dorothy's mother and father talked about how much skating meant to their little girl. They decided that if it was that important, they would see that she had what she needed to become a skater. They told her, "If this is what you want, you must work hard. We will help you."

She did work hard. Sometimes when she was waiting in the cold for her turn on the ice, she would think about what her friends were doing. They had time for games and parties. She was always at the rink. She had to go to bed early, to get up early to practice. Then she would ask herself, "Do I want those other things more than skating?" The answer was always "No."

So she practiced more and more. She went to every competition she heard about. Everyone could see that she was going to be a fine skater. Her parents did what they said they would do. Her lessons cost a lot of money. And it took time and money to travel to and from the contests in different cities.

When Dorothy was twelve, she met a skater who had been a National Champion. Her name was Sonya Dunfield. She could see that Dorothy could be a champion skater, too. Soon it was decided that Dorothy would move in with friends in New York so she could take lessons from Sonya.

She was already good. But with lessons every day, she was getting better and better. People who saw her skate talked about how good she was. At the Winter Festival in Lake Placid, she was a big hit.

Dorothy looks happy and poised on the ice.

Soon Dorothy was ready for National competition. In 1969, she flew with her coach to Seattle, Washington. This was very exciting for a twelve-year-old girl. She had worked hard for four years. That hard work was going to show. She won! Now she was Dorothy Hamill, National Champion, Novice Division.

Now she was ready to compete in the Junior Division. Dorothy spent the next summer skating in Toronto. When school started, she went back to New York. She and her coach began to get ready for the next contest. It was the Eastern Junior Ladies' Competition. And it would be held in Philadelphia in January. Dorothy had always enjoyed the free style part of the contests. She did not enjoy the school figures she had to do. But she had to make herself work on those, too. They were an important part of the program. She always did better in the free style because she enjoyed it more.

Dorothy was always nervous as she waited to go out onto the ice during a contest. Sometimes she would be so nervous she would feel sick! But she always felt at home on the ice. Her smile always broke through!

In Philadelphia, she did it again. She won the Eastern Championship!

Now it was time to begin getting ready for Nationals.

Nationals were held in Tulsa, Oklahoma in February. Dorothy was ready, but she was nervous anyway. First came the school figures. She won! She couldn't believe it! And she knew her free style program was good. Soon she was on the ice again skating to the music she had chosen. The crowd loved her. The better she skated, the more she smiled. She was beginning to be known for more than her fine skating. She was known as the girl with a smile like a flash of sunlight.

When it was all over, she had placed second. But she was only thirteen. She knew she could win next time. She said, "If I win or not, it really doesn't matter. I just do my best. As long as I know I've done that, I'm satisfied."

Now she was ready for her last test, the eighth. If she passed, she would be at the top. She would be ready to compete as a Senior Lady. She passed! All the work had paid off!

The 1971 Nationals were held in Buffalo, New York. Here she was skating in the Nationals as a Senior Lady. She won fifth place. And she was only fourteen years old!

But Dorothy won more than a place in that contest. She won the hearts of the crowd. Her red wool dress and her sparkling smile made people forget about the blizzard in Buffalo.

After the contest, some important people came to see her parents. They wanted her to go to Sopporo, Japan for the pre-Olympics! She was so excited! So were her parents. This made all the hard work seem worthwhile.

Dorothy and her mother had only four days to get ready to leave for Japan! By Wednesday morning, they were ready to go. They boarded the plane for Japan and Dorothy's first international contest. Many people left behind were excited for Dorothy, too. Her father, her brother and sister, her coach, and many friends waited to hear how she would do in a competition like this.

They were not disappointed. Soon they heard that Dorothy had taken third place at Sopporo. It was her first international competition, and she was only fourteen!

Dorothy did not make the Olympic team in 1972. She was on the alternate team and she knew four more years of hard work would make her ready. So she looked forward to the next Olympic year - 1976. It was something to work hard for.

Winning a place on the world team was so exciting for Dorothy. She was traveling and competing all over the world — Canada, France, West Germany. At age sixteen, she won the International Grand Prix in France, and the Nebelhorn Trophy in West Germany.

All the travel meant that she missed her father, brother, and sister. But her mother always traveled with her. And her father went to watch her compete every time he could. Besides, she knew that she was improving with every contest. And all the hard work was going to make her the best. She had made many sacrifices to become a good skater. After all, no teenager wants to go to bed at 8:00 and get up at 5:00! But she had to do this in order to practice seven hours a day! People asked her how she could give up so much and work so hard. She always told them, "I do it because I enjoy it. Otherwise, I would have quit long ago."

Back home at last, she talked with her parents about her goals for her life. She knew what she wanted. In Sopporo, she had met Carlo Fassi. Many people called him the greatest skating coach in the world. He had helped her before the pre-Olympics. She had always had trouble with her school figures. He had given her instructions that helped. She knew he could help her become the best skater she could be. Her parents decided that she should study with Carlo Fassi. He had a rink in Denver, Colorado where he coached skaters. He had coached Peggy Fleming before she won the Olympics in 1968.

So Dorothy moved from her home in Riverside, Connecticut. She would live, go to high school, and take lessons in Denver. Reporters asked her how she felt about being away from home. She said, "I don't like being away from home, but if I want to be a skater, that's the way it's got to be."

Coach Fassi knew that she could be the best. Once he said, "To make a champion, I have to be patient. With Dorothy, it is not always easy. She gets mad at herself."

Dorothy works out the fine points of her program.

She did get mad at herself. She wanted to do everything perfectly. She had not worked this hard for this long to be ordinary.

Dorothy's life in Denver was not easy. She went to school in the mornings. She had skating lessons and practice every afternoon. She did this six days a week. And on Sundays there were ballet lessons and exercises! All this was to help her be the best skater she could be. It was making her a strong skater. Her jumps were smooth and powerful. Her spins became flawless. She made it look so easy!

Dorothy skates her way to victory in the 1974 Nationals.

When the 1973 season opened, she was ready. She won the silver medal in the National Senior Ladies' Competition. She was getting there!

Back in Denver, Dorothy began training for the 1974 Nationals. By now she had another person to help her besides her coach. He was Bob Paul, a choreographer. Like a dancer, a skater needs music to skate by. Bob Paul helped her choose music to suit her style of skating. Together, they worked on her free-style program to make it perfect.

Dorothy still had trouble with stage fright. She was always nervous before a contest. Coach Fassi tried to help. Bob Paul tried. He told her, "Try not to think of this as anything special. Do your program as if it were a regular, everyday practice."

The 1974 Nationals began in February in Providence, Rhode Island. It was going to be hard for Dorothy to pretend that this was just another practice. Ten thousand people were watching!

Dorothy was not pleased with her school figures. She knew she could do better when her turn came again. And she did. She skated her short program to music from "Firebird." It seemed that all 10,000 loved her as they applauded.

The next night she skated well again. As she went through her program, her family and friends knew that they were watching a champion. And they were. She won the National Senior Ladies' title!

In 1974 Dorothy wins the U.S. Nationals, Kathy Malmberg comes in second, and Julie McKinstry takes third.

There was not much time to enjoy the victory. In just a month, she would be in Munich, Germany. She had to be ready for World Competition.

Going back to Europe was exciting. But Dorothy knew that she had to work hard to get her program ready in a hurry. She practiced the figures she would have to do on the first night of competition. But when the time came, she did not do them perfectly. She would have to make up for it in her free-style program.

Knowing that she had to do well made Dorothy very nervous. She was so nervous she though she could not do her program. She left the ice to speak to her coach. Then the music for her program began. She skated back onto the ice. She began to skate a perfect program. It was beautiful. All the judges gave her a score of 5-9 except one. And he gave her a perfect 6!

Even with her weak school figures, this put her up into second place. She had won the silver medal in World Competition! Dorothy came back home happy with her silver medal. But now she wanted that gold one!

Back home, Dorothy had something else to look forward to. It was something every high school student works toward. Graduation! Dorothy graduated in June from the Colorado Academy. She had looked forward to this day even more than most high school students do. Now she could spend even her mornings on ice!

She worked harder than ever after graduation. The schedule she set for herself would have been too hard for most girls. But not Dorothy. She was on the ice working every morning by seven. After a practice session, she went to exercises. After lunch she was back on the ice for an afternoon of work. She knew what she wanted. And she was willing to work hard for it.

Then a terrible thing happened. She was practicing her double axel. It was a move she did so well. But she landed wrong and hurt her foot. Later, doctors found that it needed a cast. This was terrible news for Dorothy. She was getting ready for 1975 Nationals! Now she could not skate for weeks!

Dorothy is on her way to the 1975 Nationals.

Nationals, 1976 - Dorothy wins again. Linda Fratianne is second; Wendy Burge is third.

There was nothing to do but wait for the foot to mend. It was a vacation from all the hard work. But Dorothy worried about how she would skate after the cast was off. She should not have worried. She won National Senior Ladies' again — even after being in a cast for weeks!

Now she was off to another World Competition. This time it was held at home in the U.S. — Colorado Springs. Again it was the school figures that gave her trouble. Then her short program was not her best. But she skated her free style program so well that she came from behind to win second again. She had wanted the gold this year. But after all that had happened, it was good enough for now. Besides, she knew that in a year she would be skating in the 1976 Olympics!

Early in 1976, Dorothy became National Senior Ladies' Champion again. It was the third year she had won that title. But there was no time to sit and think about that! The Olympics in Innsbruck, Austria were less than a month away!

For years Dorothy had been getting ready for this. She just did not always know it! Now there were so many things to do, even off the ice. To get ready for Innsbruck, there was music to choose. There was her program to plan. She had costumes to get ready, skates to select for each program.

People asked Dorothy if all her years of work were worth it. She always answered, "Being in the Olympics will make it all worthwhile."

Finally, it was time to go. Friends had called to wish her luck. She said to one of them, "When people say, 'Good luck in Innsbruck,' I have to pinch myself."

This time, the whole family would be there to watch Dorothy skate. After all, this was the big one. Dorothy and her mother left early to get settled in Innsbruck. Her father, her sister Marcie, her brother Sandy and his wife would arrive in time for the competition.

Opening ceremonies began February 4, 1976. During the ceremonies, Dorothy had trouble believing that she was really there. It was all too good to be true. The torch was lit. It was really going to happen. She was really here.

Before the Olympics, Dorothy relaxes with her father, (left), and Mr. and Mrs. Marshall Baker.

She had skated in competitions for eight years. She had been America's best for the last three years. Two years in a row, she had won second in World Competition. Diane de Leeuw had won first in World Competition. Diane had come to Innsbruck to win, too. Soon the world would know who was best.

At last it was time for the figure skating competition to begin. In her dressing room, Dorothy felt the nervousness she always felt before a contest. She knew why. She said, "This program will last just four minutes. But it will represent twelve years of work. I owe so much to so many people who have helped me."

Outside, reporters were talking about her. "Dorothy will light up the Olympics," one said. "Two years ago, she stole the show at Munich." She had a lot to live up to. She knew she would have to do the best she had ever done.

As she waited in her dressing room, she thought, "Am I going to fall? Why am I doing this? I'll never do it again." Suddenly, it was her turn. She had to forget the nervousness. The school figures were first. She came in second. Then she skated her short program so well she moved into first place.

After the short program, she felt numb. She said, "You're skating and doing the most difficult things and the audience is with you. They're cheering and cheering. You're floating. It's like nothing I've ever felt."

When she found that she had moved into first place, she said, "It's strange. It might really happen. I might win."

She had done all she could do. There was nothing more to do until Friday. Then she would skate her free style program.

Friday came at last. This was it. She would win or lose the Olympic gold medal in a few minutes. Waiting in her dressing room, she thought, "It's like going to an execution, — your own."

But as soon as she skated onto the ice, the fear left. Dorothy began to skate like a dancer. The crowd was silent. Then it seemed that every American in Austria began to cheer. They kept on cheering. And Dorothy Hamill kept on smiling. They threw roses and chocolates onto the ice. It was over. The Olympic gold medal was hers!

Other skaters helped her gather some of the roses from the ice. Then she skated off to where her father and her coach were waiting. There were hugs and tears as they looked at the scores — 5-8's and 5-9's.

The competition was over. It was time for the awards ceremony. Dorothy stepped to the highest level of the platform. It was still hard to believe. Then she heard the announcer say, "In third place, Christine Errath of East Germany. In second place, Diane de Leeuw of the Netherlands. And in first place, Dorothy Hamill of the United States."

She heard her own national anthem being played. She knew that "The Star Spangled Banner" was being played for her. Tears were shining in her eyes. But her smile sparkled like sunlight on the ice. She would never forget this moment. No one who saw it would ever forget it.

Later when Dorothy went to the celebration dinner, she took the gold medal with her. It was hard to tell who was happier — Dorothy, her family, or her coach. The celebration lasted all night. Dorothy Hamill, Olympic Champion, went to bed at 5:00 in the morning! The gold medal was under her pillow as she slept.

Everywhere she went now, people knew her. They wanted to ask her questions. They wanted her autograph. The question asked most often was "What are you going to do now?" She would have to think about that. Now she was going to get some rest.

A month later, she skated in the World Competition in Sweden. She took home the gold medal there, too. She also took home a mink coat she bought in Sweden.

Dorothy holds the medal she has worked for all her life.

Finally she was back home in Riverside. Family friends greeted her with a parade. They were so proud of their hometown girl! Her old high school, Greenwich High, gave her an honorary diploma. They showed films of her Olympic performance. At home the phones never stopped ringing. Mail arrived all during the day. There were presents and telegrams. Reporters, T.V. cameras, movie and magazine people were all over the place. There was no end to the excitement.

All the time, Dorothy was thinking about what she would do now. She had movie offers. She was wanted for magazine ads and TV commercials. Even her hairdo was famous! She had some very important decisions to make.

There was one offer she thought about the most. It was from Ice Capades. Dorothy decided to sign a contract with them. Everyone wanted to see the Olympic champion skate in the Ice Capades. She would draw crowds for the tour. She also signed a contract with ABC TV to do two special shows. She said, "I chose ABC because they were so nice to me at the Olympics."

Dorothy hired a friend, Kim Danks, as her secretary to help her with all the mail that kept coming in.

Dorothy looked forward to her new life. She said, "I'll be skating for people, not judges."

There was some time for fun now. On a trip to California, she met Henry Winkler, "the Fonz."

She found time to be with her boyfriend in Colorado Springs. She had met him at a rink where she practiced.

After a full summer, it was time to begin her tour with Ice Capades. When the show opened, Dorothy found that even an Olympic champion can be nervous. Eight thousand people waited in Pittsburgh to see the Olympic champ. She was eager to put on a good show. She skated out onto the ice in a white dress trimmed in red, white and blue. The crowd cheered. Before she began to skate, she spoke to the audience. "I'd like to take a moment to say hello to you," she said. "I'm happy to be with the Ice Capades." Then she began to skate the program that had won the gold medal. She started strong as always. Suddenly, she fell. "Oh, my," the crowd heard her say. But she finished her program. She gave the crowd what they came to see. They loved her. They stood up and cheered just as they had done at Innsbruck.

After the show, she talked about the fall. "Just because you win the Olympics doesn't mean you don't fall," she said. "You can't do everything right all the time."

Dorothy Hamill, at age twenty, has done more things right than most people do in a lifetime. More than half her life has been spent training and working hard to get where she is today. And the people love her for it. They love her skating. They love her shyness. They adore her bright smile. Girls copy her hairdo. And they keep coming to see her skate even if she falls now and then. Dorothy Hamill is the girl next door who became an Olympic champion.

Dorothy at home with her collection of dolls and animals.

If You Enjoyed

DOROTHY HAMILL
SKATE TO VICTORY

Then Don't Miss Reading

FRAN TARKENTON
MASTER OF THE GRIDIRON

MUHAMMAD ALI
THE GREATEST

O. J. SIMPSON
THE JUICE IS LOOSE

CHRIS EVERT
WOMEN'S TENNIS CHAMPION

EVEL KNIEVEL
MOTORCYCLE DAREDEVIL

from

CRESTWOOD HOUSE

P.O. BOX 3427   MANKATO, MINNESOTA 56001

Write Us for a Complete Catalog